WENT THE DAY WELL?

....

Penelope Houston

BFI PUBLISHING

First published in 1992 by the
BRITISH FILM INSTITUTE
21 Stephen Street, London W1P 1PL

Reprinted 1993

British Library Cataloguing in Publication Data

Houston, Penelope
    Went the day well?
    I. Title
    791.4372

ISBN 0–85170–318–6

Designed by
Andrew Barron & Collis Clements Associates

Typesetting by
Fakenham Photosetting Limited, Norfolk

Printed in Great Britain by
The Trinity Press, Worcester

CONTENTS

....

Went the day well?
We died and never knew.
But, well or ill,
Freedom, we died for you.

ACKNOWLEDGMENTS

A number of people have helped me with my research into *Went the Day Well?* I would like to thank particularly Diana Morgan and Sidney Cole, for being so generous with their time and their memories of the film. I am grateful also to Michael Relph, Monja Danischewsky, Anthony Aldgate, Charles Barr and Quentin Falk for information and advice; and to Ray Stockings of Weintraub Entertainment, which now owns the rights in the Ealing films, for looking out useful documentation, including the film's dialogue sheets. Thanks also to my British Film Institute colleagues Elaine Burrows and Jackie Morris, of the National Film Archive Viewing Service, and David Sharp, of Library Services, for their helpfulness.

Publication details of books quoted in the text are given in the Bibliography. Other quotations are from the microfiche on the film in the BFI library; from the wartime Ministry of Information files now in the Public Record Office at Kew; and from Sir Michael Balcon's papers, deposited in the BFI library. Quotations from the Balcon papers are printed by kind permission of Jonathan Balcon. The credits for *Went the Day Well?* were compiled by Markku Salmi. Illustrations are from the Stills, Posters and Designs Department of the BFI.

Invasion in Miss Marple country

INTRODUCTION

· ·

When I signed on to write about *Went the Day Well?* for this series, I was envisaging a fairly straightforward assignment. *Went the Day Well?* is not by any reasonable standard of measurement a major film, but it belongs with those minor ones which so regularly manage to outperform and outstay many of their seeming betters. Rather surprisingly, it was the only British feature film made during the war to deal seriously – if perhaps in the long run not all that seriously – with the prospect of invasion, to show British civilians coming to grips on home ground with the German army. It combines an underlying sense of essential security with an unpredictable edge of ruthlessness: it is not a comfortable picture. Although the film is set in the most secure of English country landscapes, the very heart of Miss Marple country, it finds the plump postmistress and the scatter-brained landgirl capable of fighting ferociously in defence of their own. The German parachutists who have the ill luck to turn up in Bramley End never really stand a chance.

Went the Day Well? was the first feature directed in England by Alberto Cavalcanti, the dynamic Brazilian who had served as *eminence* not at all *grise* of British documentary during the 1930s and then moved on to play the same sort of role at Michael Balcon's Ealing Studios. It came at a time when British film-makers in general, and those at Ealing in particular, were trying to assimilate the lessons of documentary into feature production, as a way of bringing a necessary realism into their treatment of war. And it was made during a period of considerable difficulty for British cinema, with many of the actors in uniform, studios threatened with requisition, production in sharp decline. A studio chief of Balcon's exemplary obstinacy felt at times that he was at war not only with the Germans but with the British government.

These are all good reasons for being interested in *Went the Day Well?*, but this is not a film of any striking depth or subtlety. What you see, on the whole, is what you get. There are few puzzles of interpretation to be tracked down. Not, that is, in the film itself. I jotted down a dozen or so factual questions about its production history, innocently assuming that these would be quite easily answered.

Not so easy, however. The day-to-day studio records would seem at some time to have been junked. There are few paper trails to follow; no Ealing archive nesting securely in some university, as is the case with so many of the American studios. Sir Michael Balcon's great store of personal papers, now in the British Film Institute library, is an invaluable source, but not always too informative when it comes to individual titles. In trying to discover just how and when the script came to be written, or at what point Cavalcanti involved himself in the project, I found minor queries beginning to look like tantalising puzzles.

At the end of the day, I managed to answer most of the key questions, although not the one which is perhaps the most intriguing. But the process of delving into the circumstances of a film involves, in itself, much shifting of perspective. Alternatives appear: the film with another title, perhaps, or with a different cast. There is also a copy of the shooting script in the BFI library, and inevitably it opens up more areas of choice. Did they actually shoot that sequence which is no longer in the picture? Why did they make the story seem more perplexing than it needed to be, by cutting rather basic information contained in the original dialogue? Why does Marie Lohr die in the film when the shooting script allows her to survive? And there is a further question, likely to be at the back of one's mind when looking at these British war films, of how far there may have been a deliberate propaganda purpose. Did the government find it timely, in 1942, to remind the public that the threat of invasion had not entirely disappeared?

The more one looks into a film, I suspect, the more elusive it begins to appear. Something ended up on the screen; and it perhaps had not too close a connection to what anyone had in mind at the outset. *Went the Day Well?* seems a case in point. In one sense, the film needs no explanation; in another, the answers are in the circumstances of its making. The anonymous reviewer in *Documentary News Letter* noted that its faults were 'many, frequent and completely unimportant'. If the reviewer was Basil Wright, as seems at least worth a guess, it's not surprising that the judgment still looks pretty sound, fifty years later.

1
STORYLINES
· ·

Went the Day Well? opens in a quiet English country churchyard. 'Come to have a look at Bramley End, have you?' asks the verger, waiting to waylay us with all the determination of an inveterate storyteller. We're there, he tells us, because of the German names recorded on a little war memorial. 'They wanted England, these Jerries did, and this is the only bit they got.' Immediately, he dives into reminiscence: 'It was Saturday morning when those army lorries came rumbling along the road from Upton. We'd have laughed at you if you'd told us we'd got a real live German right under our very noses and we'd have thought you was a bit weak in the upper storey if you'd said the chaps in those lorries was anything else but ordinary British tommies. Pretty soon we learned better ...' Before he has finished speaking, the camera moves away from the churchyard to pick up the small convoy advancing along the road into Bramley End.

The war is over, the verger (Mervyn Johns) has told us. Bramley End has long since returned to its tranquil self. A film which went into

'A quiet English country churchyard'

production during the dark days of early 1942, weeks after the fall of Singapore, months before El Alamein, had the assurance, even cheek, to look so confidently to the future, soothing its audience before getting down to the business of unsettling them. I had sometimes wondered whether this prologue was actually an afterthought, perhaps tacked on to the picture after the rest had been shot, by which time optimism could have been more justified. But it's there already in the shooting script, dated 28 March 1942.

The flashback action tells of a village under enemy occupation for two days, the Whitsun weekend of 1942. The men who arrive in the lorries are German parachutists, sixty of them, passing themselves off as Royal Engineers and demanding billets in the village while they carry out an exercise in the area. The villagers may be deceived by the friendly uniforms, but there is no attempt to bamboozle the audience. Ortler (Basil Sydney), the German C.O., almost immediately makes contact with Oliver Wilsford (Leslie Banks), a respectable resident who is also the 'real live German under our very noses', no mere Nazi sympathiser or fifth columnist but an agent taking his orders from

(left to right) Valerie Taylor, C. V. France, Leslie Banks, Basil Sydney

Berlin. Ortler's task is to jam the British radio-location over a three hundred mile area and to protect the equipment. If necessary, he and his men are to hold the village for forty-eight hours.

The Germans settle into their billets, but rather carelessly manage to arouse a few suspicions. The vicar's daughter, Nora (Valerie Taylor), in particular wonders why Royal Engineers should be writing their sevens in the continental way and how a slab of Austrian chocolate has found its way into the kit of 'Major Hammond' (Ortler). Wilsford heads her off, but alerts Ortler to put 'Plan B' into operation. The lanes are barricaded and walkers and cyclists turned away. Those villagers not already in church are herded there ('But we're chapel,' objects one perplexed local). The vicar is shot when he tries to ring the church bells as a warning. Later, four men cycling back after a Home Guard exercise are ambushed and mown down.

Given half a chance, the villagers do their unavailing best to send messages to the outside world. At night, however, there are two successful escape attempts. George (Harry Fowler), a resourceful young evacuee billeted at the manor house, shins down a drainpipe and makes contact in the woods with his friend Bill Purvis (Edward Rigby), the local poacher. Purvis kills one German but is shot while staging a diversion. George, with a bullet wound in his leg, staggers to the next village to alert the Home Guard: 'Jerries at Bramley'. Meanwhile, Tom Sturry (Frank Lawton), son of the village publican and on leave from the navy for his wedding, leads a break-out from the church, recaptures the post office and telephones for help. Sturry and his small force head for the manor house, to rescue the children held hostage there and to hold it until the army arrives. Wilsford, still unsuspected by everyone except Nora and the lady of the manor, is shot dead by Nora as he is pulling down the barricades to let the Germans into the manor. The villagers hold out; the army and the Home Guard arrive in strength; the Battle of Bramley End is over.

Went the Day Well? (or, as it was then called, *They Came in Khaki*) went into production on 26 March 1942 on Stage 2 at Ealing: 'INT. VICARAGE DINING ROOM AND HALL'. Twenty-one months earlier, on 29 June 1940, a story by Graham Greene called *The Lieutenant Died Last* had been published in the American magazine *Collier's*, 'the national weekly'. The film is 'based on' this story, although a good many things happened to it along the way.

Graham Greene's village has none of the cooking apple cosiness of Bramley End (Bramley Green in the shooting script and also, oddly, in some of the first reviews). He gives it the uncompromisingly dismal name of Potter and locates it precisely: 'One of those tiny isolated villages you still find dumped down in deserted corners of what we call in England "Metroland" – the district where commuters live in tidy villas within easy distances of the railway, on the edge of scrubby commons full of clay pits and gorse and rather withered trees.' To get there, 'You take a turning marked "No Through Road" and bump heavily towards what looks like a farm gate stuck a mile or more over the shaggy common. Through the gate is nothing but Potter ...'

Potter is not pretty; its church is not thirteenth-century but tin-roofed twentieth-century; its inhabitants are a grumbling, fractious lot. But it is within miles of the main-line railway, and when the German parachutists arrive (only about ten, rather than the sixty the film allows to tumble unobserved from the sky), their purpose is to sabotage the railway. They are wearing their own uniforms, which ensures them prisoner of war status if captured, and they behave in a rather more businesslike way than Ortler and his troop.

The villagers are rounded up in the pub. 'The post office is closed,' says its guardian, when the German officer turns up on her doorstep. 'She didn't think he looked like a shop customer,' even though he calls her 'madam'. The telephone wires have prudently been cut. There is hardly any deliberate violence, and the one village casualty is a boy who tries to make a run for it. 'They had fired, humanely, at his legs; but he was crippled for life.'

Out in the woods, the poacher, Bill Purves (*sic*), has been going about his own affairs and actually seen the parachutists coming down. ' "It didn't seem right," he said afterwards; he meant that it didn't seem fair, people peeking at you like that out of the sky.' He is none too clear about just what war is going on: ' "The bloody Bojers," Purves said aloud, the old brain creaking rustily back forty years to South Africa and an ambush on the veldt.' But he stalks the Germans, catches them on the railway line, finds the hunt 'more fun than rabbit shooting'. He gets several of the Germans, before one of his shots sets off the explosives they are planting and does for the rest. Purves feels a bit sickened: it was 'like dynamiting fish'. The German lieutenant, fatally injured, appeals to Purves to finish him off; which he does, as he would any wounded animal. And he takes from the lieutenant's pocket a photograph of a baby.

Purves is not particularly thanked by anyone for his rather spectacular role in checking the invasion; merely let off with a caution when caught with the rabbits in his poacher's pocket. 'One souvenir he never showed to anyone – the photograph of the baby on the mat. Sometimes he took it out of a drawer and looked at it himself – uneasily. It made him – for no reason that he could understand – feel bad.'

Graham Greene's story is very short: a mere half-dozen magazine columns. It's an odd, sardonic little tale, very exact in its description, elusive in its attitudes. It might even have been subjected to some of that ruthless American style-editing: 'feel bad' doesn't sound quite right, for an elderly English poacher in 1940, and the dashes that break out like a rash over the story's last three sentences don't look right. The interesting questions, however, are how *The Lieutenant Died Last* came to be published where it did, and what happened to it before Ealing signed a contract for making a film based on the story, which they did not do until February 1942.

Anthony Aldgate, it seems to me, has answered the first question as satisfactorily as anyone is likely to do, in his interesting chapter on *Went the Day Well?* in *Britain Can Take It*. Although Graham Greene's war service at the Ministry of Information was brief, he was certainly there in April 1940, Aldgate points out, 'as one of the two specialists in Branch II (Literature)'. I came across an MoI minute which seems to indicate that he was still there in August 1940, when according to the dates given to Aldgate by Greene's agent, Gerald Pollinger, he should have been well away. In the summer of 1940, as Aldgate says, the Ministry's Policy Committee 'was greatly exercised with thoughts and ideas on how best to project Britain's cause and case in America.' The *Collier's* connection would appear to have been launched with publication of the Greene story, a tasty enough morsel to dangle before an editor. It was strengthened later in 1940, when Quentin Reynolds, the magazine's London correspondent, wrote and narrated the commentary for *London Can Take It,* the blitz documentary which did so much for Britain's 'cause and case' in America.

There seem solid grounds for backing Aldgate's theory: *The Lieutenant Died Last* probably landed in *Collier's* because the Ministry of Information managed to place it there. Aldgate tucks away in a footnote an assurance from Gerald Pollinger that 'the story was not written under any kind of official pressure as propaganda' and that 'Graham Greene says he has never written any fiction under official guidance, and this applies to this story.'

It remains quite possible, however, that the story could have been published as propaganda, with Greene's approval, but actually written with no such intention. If Graham Greene had set out to write something calculated to persuade *Collier's* middle-American readership of Britain's worth, it's hard to believe that he (or, indeed, almost anyone) could not have done a little better than *The Lieutenant Died Last.* Admittedly, a semi-senile village reprobate gets the better of a German platoon; and one can make a case, as Aldgate does, for the telling effects of 'English understatement' and the like. But what would American readers have made of Potter, that sulky little place where they are so befuddled by ARP and AFS uniforms that they can't recognise a German one, where there appear to be no warning or defence systems, and where the villagers, meek though surly, fit compliantly into the German scheme of things? Any support for a Britain made up of Potters, they might well have felt, would be support wasted.

It is unlikely that *Collier's* would have been widely read in Britain, and Greene's story was not picked up by any British paper or magazine. Ealing, for its part, was not a studio with a large story department, acquiring and stockpiling material. The initiative to buy a story would come, as a general practice, from the creative people. So how did the studio get to hear of *The Lieutenant Died Last,* of which they were to keep so little in the film? (The notion of parachutists taking over an English village; the character of the old poacher, with his role considerably changed but his name, rather touchingly, left virtually intact.)

Here the cat has been thrown somewhat among the pigeons by Michael Balcon. His autobiography, *A Lifetime of Films,* allows only one short paragraph to *Went the Day Well?* and that paragraph contains only one factual statement. Cavalcanti's film 'was based on an original story by his friend Graham Greene, who also worked on the script.' Balcon's book is a disappointingly flat and unimaginative piece of writing from a complex and imaginative man. It gives an impression of having been written close to his files, hugging the facts as one might hug the road.

But did Graham Greene work on the script, and if so how much and when? That was the puzzle I was unable to solve. Monja Danischewsky, who was head of publicity at Ealing at the time, told me that if Greene had spent any time at the studio, the event would surely have been 'painted on my memory'. It isn't. Quentin Falk interviewed Greene while writing *Travels in Greeneland*, about the novelist's many involvements with the cinema. There is no suggestion in the book that Greene had anything to do with the script of *Went the Day Well?*, and Falk confirmed to me that he was given no inkling of this during their conversation. Greene's comments to Falk, in fact, are on the testy side. 'I was in Africa when it came out. My sister saw it on television recently and didn't like it at all.' He leaves the impression that he would have preferred both his own title and his own story: 'The whole story is practically seen through the eyes of the old poacher as he stalks them with his shotgun ...'

A tidy and elegant theory can be worked out, which fits the pieces together in the most appealing way. Graham Greene and Cavalcanti were certainly friends. Norman Sherry in his biography of Greene quotes a prewar letter in which there was already mention of a possible collaboration between them. Cavalcanti, a newcomer to Ealing and to British feature production, might well have been casting about for appropriate material with a war setting. Greene might have suggested his own story as a possibility, and together they might have roughed out some script ideas. Short though the story is, it could certainly have made a film, although it would have demanded scripting altogether more rigorous and observant than Ealing's usual rather scattershot methods. And Greene's almost irritable references to a film he never saw would make better sense if he still had in mind the different kind of film he had once actually set out to make.

At some point, the project could have been shelved – Greene went abroad, Cavalcanti became caught up in another picture, the studio lost interest. At some later stage, the Ealing house writers,

Angus MacPhail and John Dighton, would have taken over and constructed a new story out of the bones of the material, and one that showed the villagers in an altogether more active and attractive light. Later still, the point at which we return to fairly firm ground, the third writer, Diana Morgan, was brought in. 'I went over and found this script which was almost ready to be done,' she told me. 'And it was unplayable. I think that's the word. They knew it was, and that's why they sent for me. It was all a fearful muddle. The story was there, the action was there, but the people weren't. They were just names. And what I really did was make them into parts for the actors and make them actable scenes.' At the time she became involved, she remembers, she had to work quickly, with rewrites still going on during shooting.

But until the entry of Diana Morgan, the rest is entirely conjecture, a theory without a shred of evidence to support it. Interestingly, Diana Morgan told me that although she knew the script was based on a Graham Greene story, which gave it a certain cachet, she had never read *The Lieutenant Died Last*, and had no idea where story and script parted company. She came in late, as was so often the case, took what she was given to work with, and had no time for curiosity about what might have existed before.

I had been reluctant to approach Graham Greene directly. Anything he had been quoted as saying about the film suggested that he found the subject boring, if anything rather annoying. There seemed little likelihood of getting straight answers. I had hoped that Diana Morgan might be able to fill in the missing piece of the puzzle, but I drove away from my meeting with her thinking that it would have after all to be the direct approach, and contemplating the kind of questions that might actually hope to attract answers. I was almost home when I saw the first of the London *Evening Standard* posters: 'Graham Greene Dead'. Regret was tempered by a sense that fate had taken over, providing the dramatically right conclusion to a search which, I had been feeling for some time, was never going to result in anything as prosaic as a positive answer.

The Lieutenant Died Last did not make it into Graham Greene's *Collected Short Stories*, but was included in *The Last Word and Other Stories* (1990), along with another story left over from the war, *The News in English*. 'I am taking the risk of reprinting,' Greene wrote, 'because I like the stories, and my friend Cavalcanti made a film of *The Lieutenant Died Last* which I regret never having seen, for I was out of England on wartime duties when it was shown.' Neither his regret nor his curiosity can have gone very deep. He had, after all, some forty years to catch up with *Went the Day Well?*, if he had been so minded.

2
GERMANS IN THE BACK GARDEN
....

Charles Barr's *Ealing Studios* is a fine and illuminating book. Barr, however, makes an odd, highly uncharacteristic error in the dating of *Went the Day Well?* He has the shooting date right but the opening precisely a year out, October 1943 against, correctly, October 1942; which in turn throws his chronological list of Ealing productions out of step. When authoritative sources slip, unfortunately, others slide after them. Both George Perry's *Forever Ealing* and Quentin Falk's *Travels in Greeneland* give the 1943 date. In writing to Sidney Cole, who edited the film, I suggested that he must have had to work quickly, even for those

The Next of Kin: commandos erect a barrier during street fighting

19

days, given that *Went the Day Well?* opened in London a bare four months after the end of shooting. Cole was perplexed. He remembered that he had indeed worked at speed, but had checked his own reference books and couldn't understand why this should have been necessary. In view of all this, it seems as well to state categorically that *Went the Day Well?* was first press shown at the end of October 1942, at the old London Pavilion cinema.

Barr is entirely right, it seems to me, in linking *Went the Day Well?* with *The Foreman Went to France* and *The Next of Kin*, two war films from Ealing released earlier in the same year. (Although *Next of Kin*, being directed by the 'outsider' Thorold Dickinson, never quite fitted into the Ealing canon.) The three films work as a 'loose trilogy', Barr suggests, in which 'the threat of an enemy who may be all around enforces resource and alertness and penalises complacency and amateurism.' There are even some links of structure and style, which Barr understandably doesn't mention, between *The Foreman Went to France*, on which Cavalcanti was associate producer, and *Went the Day Well?*, which he directed. And in all three films there is the warning that people may not be as they seem, that authority is not necessarily to be depended on. Mistrust has to be learned.

Of the three, *The Next of Kin* stands out as the film which sees most clearly just where it intends to go and also the surest way of getting there. The War Office had initially approached Ealing to make a service training film on the subject of security, and put up £20,000. The studio expanded the production to feature length, more than doubled its budget out of their own resources, and survived a well-documented history of brushes and disagreements with the services and a pre-release bout with the Prime Minister. Interestingly, as Jeffrey Richards records in *Britain Can Take It*, the first story treatment had 'the threatened invasion of Britain' as a background. The War Office turned this down, and the film instead builds towards a British raid on the French coast, which the Germans are able to anticipate thanks to the work of a spy ring and information picked up from careless talk. The agents' task is made a little easier by British complacency and reluctance to ask awkward questions. To the trade press, while it was shooting and afterwards, *The Next of Kin* was Ealing's 'hush-hush film'.

The film's strongest card is probably the clarity and momentum of its script. Angus MacPhail, head of Ealing's story department, and John Dighton worked on it, along with Thorold Dickinson and also Sir Basil Bartlett, who was both an intelligence officer and a playwright. Dickinson was always a film-maker with a strong sense of structure. The MacPhail/Dighton scripts tend to slam all sorts of incidents together, risking collisions and traffic jams. But in this case the links of the chain which in effect makes up the action are not allowed to slacken, the connections are made and they all function properly. A sustained trajectory carries the film towards the climax of the raid: not a failure (that would have been more than the public could have taken at that stage of the war), but achieving its objective at the cost of unnecessarily heavy casualties.

The enemy agents include a quiet little Welshman, a theatre dresser, a provincial bookseller whose shop seems unusually heavily stocked with left-wing texts from Gollancz: not at all the usual bumbling and Heiling bunch of the early war films. At the end, Charters and Caldicott, once again on a train, are showing off to each other about some scrap of service gossip. A helpful hand offers a cigarette lighter. It's the very unobtrusive, very efficient Welsh agent, still at large and still listening. He was played, of course, by Mervyn Johns, Ealing's indispensable actor of those days, who actually appears in all three films.

The Foreman Went to France, directed by Charles Frend, is taken from a story by J. B. Priestley which was founded on fact. During the fall of France, a factory foreman (another Welshman, Clifford Evans) worries about the fate of two precious machines which have been lent to a business in France, and moves heaven, earth and the Passport Office in his determination to make a solo expedition to rescue them. This he eventually does, joining forces along the way with an American secretary (Constance Cummings) and enlisting a stray British army lorry and its crew, cockney sparrow Tommy Trinder and wistful Scot Gordon Jackson.

This is a film in which everyone in authority behaves badly. The gallant foreman's British bosses are merely lazy and complacent. The French government has guaranteed the security of the machines, what more can he want and why can't he stop making a nuisance of himself? French officials are uniformly duplicitous and treacherous, if not worse.

At his destination, the foreman confides his errand to the station-master, who promptly tips off the local mayor, a notorious fifth columnist. The mayor (an almost lissom Robert Morley) is easily thwarted in his efforts to prevent the foreman from making off with the machines, but in another town another oily official steers the party into a trap involving a bogus British officer (John Williams, later to be Hitchcock's favourite quintessential Englishman).

The film's message is packed into a 'Wake Up, England' speech from the foreman and its not entirely persuasive denouement. When the lorry eventually grinds its way to a small harbour town, the only ship sailing is already laden with refugees and their possessions. The skipper will only take the machines if the French agree to jettison their precious things. Until this point, the foreman has shown the utmost resolution about bringing his load home, but now he rather meekly agrees to abide by their decision. And the refugees, after only the most perfunctory show of Gallic shrugging and pouting, vote in favour of the machines. It was very much in the line of Priestley's thinking, and of Ealing's, that 'ordinary people', left on their own, could be depended on to do the right and patriotic thing. It would be a few years before Ealing

John Williams (back to camera), Tommy Trinder and Gordon Jackson in *The Foreman Went to France*

decided that ordinary people, left on their own, were as likely to be found protecting illicit whisky supplies from the law or setting up independent states in the heart of London.

'What made *The Foreman Went to France* noteworthy was Cavalcanti's influence,' Balcon wrote in his autobiography, 'as for the first time he agreed to become my associate producer on one of our feature films.' He was 'wonderful on the film'. It is interesting that the film shares with *Went the Day Well?* both its flashback structure and some of those sudden swings of mood which were liable to turn up in any MacPhail/Dighton script. Impressively strong scenes, such as the strafing of the refugees on the road by German planes or the arrival at a devastated town, are slammed up against larky adventures with opponents who are much too easily outwitted; and, of course, Tommy Trinder's incessantly amiable London bus conductor patter. Which does not, by any means, indicate that the film is ineffectual: it is carried along by a kind of careless energy, a determination to keep going and get there, like the progress across France of its own jolting lorry.

Went the Day Well? could be described, in a sense, as another Ealing hush-hush film. Towards the end of 1941, and early in 1942, the studio announced its production plans for the coming year. Its mind would seem to have been running on resistance themes. There was to be a film about 'the Abyssinian revolt', involving Cavalcanti as associate producer; *V* or *Revolt*, about the French resistance; and *Chetnik*, to be scripted by Monja Danischewsky, set in Yugoslavia and shot in Wales. There is no mention in any of these plans of *Went the Day Well?*

Chetnik eventually surfaced in July 1943 as *Undercover*, after many vicissitudes, including a change of British government policy (to backing Tito) which took place, as it were, in mid-script. The Abyssinian film was still being mentioned as late as October 1942, but was not otherwise heard of again. *V* was the work of 'Francis Beeding' (pseudonym of Hilary St George Saunders and John Palmer), now probably remembered, if at all, as author of *The House of Dr Edwardes*, the novel on which Hitchcock's *Spellbound* was based. In the Balcon papers there is a memo by Robert Hamer which takes the *V* project fairly comprehensively apart, suggesting script problems. So the disappearance from immediate studio plans both of this film and of the Abyssinian story may have opened the door for Cavalcanti's picture. It was only in mid-February 1942 that a forthcoming production tentatively titled *They Came in Khaki* received a brief mention in the trade press. A few weeks later it had become a 'tribute to the Home Guard' and by 31 March Leslie Banks had joined the cast.

Why, at this particular stage in the war, did Ealing choose to go ahead with a film on an invasion theme? In *Britain Can Take It*, Anthony Aldgate develops an argument which so far, he admits, he has been unable to substantiate. In February 1942, in what was regarded in Britain as the 'blackest week since Dunkirk', a Ministry of Information Home Intelligence report suggested that 'many people are now . . . taking the possibility of invasion seriously.' There was a renewed demand for 'clarification of the role of the civilian in the event of invasion'. Within a few weeks, dependable Ealing had put *Went the Day Well?* into production – though they could hardly have done so if the film had not already reached a fairly advanced stage of preparation.

'It is difficult to escape the conclusion that it was, in effect, an "official" film,' Aldgate writes, 'and that it carried the MoI stamp of approval. . . . It bore the hallmarks of an MoI production and it marked the culmination of a long invasion propaganda campaign, though that was by no means the only campaign to which it alluded. In fact, the film was in many respects a summation of a good deal of MoI thinking, and it neatly encapsulated much of what the MoI stood for by 1942.'

(One of the 'regular visual allusions' Aldgate finds to other MoI campaigns concerns the 'be like Dad, keep Mum' poster on a wall of the village hall. In the shooting script, it was to serve a characteristically joky purpose. Why this exhortation to the younger generation, one German soldier asks another. 'Because the male members are decadent, they shirk the man's duty to support the woman.')

A trawl through the Ministry of Information papers in the Public Record Office produces no mention of the film; not surprising, since records of the Ministry's cooperation with commercial companies would seem generally not to have survived. The minutes of the MoI Planning Committee for 1941–2 certainly reveal repeated discussions about how the invasion danger should be presented to the public, along with plans for films on such subjects as the wartime role of carrier pigeons and on soup-making and carrots (the latter vetoed: 'it was felt that the public was tired of being told about carrots'). In a July 1941 paper, it was precisely suggested that people should be advised to think of invasion not necessarily as action on a grand scale but in terms of 'airborne men and equipment which may land in small groups to cause alarm and to interrupt communications. ... If they [the public] were suddenly to find Germans in their back gardens, there might be a slight danger of panic.' On 29 January 1942, they were still discussing how far, if at all, civilians should be instructed to take independent action against invasion forces. 'Don't scorch the earth without orders,' notes the paper.

All this, however, had to do with leaflet publicity, not with films. And Balcon, in any case, did not love the MoI. In December 1940 a Planning Committee minute recorded, without comment, that he had refused to make *Blockade* (*The Big Blockade*) with the MoI and was instead working with the Ministry of Economic Warfare. In the same month a trade press story from Ealing noted: 'It is an odd thing to say of a government department [MoI] that it has hampered the war effort of an independent commercial concern.' Only Balcon could have taken a position at once so rational and so lordly. Ealing even issued its own kind of ultimatum, announcing that it could no longer produce propaganda films for the Ministry. All in all, one is left with the impression that Balcon found the MoI more trying, if anything, than the Germans.

In December 1941, in terms of the film industry in general, he was talking of 'an almost impassable barrier [erected, in effect, by the government] which defeats every attempt to make the best use of our resources'. And as late as January 1943 he complained in a letter to *The Times*: 'At no time has the government given us a lead in what it has required. ... Such national propaganda as emerged from the industry was made entirely on its own initiative and certainly without an overall national scheme of propaganda.' The service film units, he then felt, were being afforded unfair advantages: 'The record of the commercial industry, deflated and technically impoverished, is higher.'

Much of Balcon's time in these years was taken up with industry policy meetings, negotiations with the government, efforts to keep an embattled and often unhappy industry afloat. National production had fallen from some 200 titles annually in the prewar years to a mere thirty-nine in 1941. There were severe shortages of manpower and of studio space; at one time in 1942 nationalisation seemed to loom as a possibility. And Balcon's stubborn insistence on pursuing the 'war effort of an independent commercial concern' did not necessarily win him friends in the industry and was sometimes doubted within his own studio. Ealing's war films earned more prestige than money; there would always be suggestions that the public wanted, even deserved, a more relaxing brand of entertainment. If *Went the Day Well?* lacks the stern logic of *The Next of Kin*, for instance, Sidney Cole suggested that one reason might even have been a reaction to criticism of the earlier film as simply too grim, too effective, too frightening.

In any case, one of the hazards of using feature films for propaganda purposes was the time it took to get a picture on the screen. The war moved on; campaign emphases changed, often abruptly and unpredictably. If in March 1942 the MoI would have welcomed an invasion film, by October it would have lost interest; and everyone involved could have foreseen that this might well happen. If *Went the Day Well?* was in some sense an 'official' film, as Anthony Aldgate suggests, neither Sidney Cole nor Diana Morgan knew anything about it – though they both left some options open.

Sidney Cole reminded me that this was, as it remains, a small industry. Everyone knew everyone else, and everyone knew Jack Beddington of the MoI Films Division. A casual suggestion over lunch might have been more effective than a formal request in getting a film off the ground or a particular policy stressed. I asked Diana Morgan whether anyone had suggested any guidelines to follow, any special points about civilian conduct to put across. 'Not a thing. But then, it wouldn't have reached us hacks.' She added that there was usually an adviser on a picture: 'I don't remember one on this film, but he was probably lurking somewhere. We thought they were only there to check the uniforms, but they may have been there for something else.'

Her own suggestion as to why *Went the Day Well?* turned up in the Ealing schedule at that particular moment is more down-to-earth and, if only for that reason, more probable: 'I think the studio was rather like the BBC. They like something; they accept it; and then they put it on the shelf and do something else. Then a slot suddenly appears and they think, what have we got? Oh yes, there's that thing Cav was so keen on. So they get it out and look at it, and they think ... well,

Mervyn Johns is available ... we can always get so and so ... let's do that. And then it's all a rush. I think that is all there was to it.'

In any event, although the film's theme is an attempted invasion, and the way the village conducts itself under extreme pressure, there are not too many lessons in it for the public to pick up – other than general 'have a go' principles. Germans suddenly appearing in the back garden might still create 'a slight danger of panic'. In some ways, the film's most interesting propaganda aspect, and the obvious link with its two Ealing predecessors, is the emphasis on the enemy within, the betrayers who wear the uniform of trusted authority.

Like *The Next of Kin*, *Went the Day Well?* is a film without a central character; except that *The Next of Kin* does very well without such a character, whereas Wilsford might be seen as the missing centre of *Went the Day Well?* He remains a curiously blank and puzzling presence, as though the film had never quite made up its mind how to deal with him. The most significant thing about him, of course, is that he is a German agent, and the shooting script was a good deal more explicit about this. In an early exchange with Ortler, he explains that he has been 'officially British' since 1935 ('a little matter of faking one's passport and one's birth certificate'). Later, the line 'I'm glad I'm justifying my seven years exile' has been cut. Wilsford is instead told that he may get an Iron Cross for his efforts. Whether by accident or design, by casual cuts or deliberate fudging, or even because Leslie Banks' bland, tweedy, very English style imposed itself too thoroughly on the character, the film itself seems to forget just who Wilsford is. The 'real live German' reference in the prologue is about the only reminder of his origins; and this line, intriguingly, is *not* in the shooting script. Presumably it was added as a trade-off for the more explicit references that have gone missing.

Most reviewers have described Wilsford as 'the squire', whatever exactly that may be taken to mean. They have their justification within the film: 'After all he's done for the village, he ought to be a brigadier at least,' gushes poor Nora, all too evidently smitten with the man she will later have to kill. But his own local power base is in the Home Guard, and the two centres of village authority would seem to remain the traditional ones – manor house and vicarage, with some tensions between them. Mrs Fraser (Marie Lohr), the lady of the manor, in her own eyes certainly runs the village. And it is Mrs Fraser, incidentally, who suggests that Wilsford should be their spokesman in dealings with the Germans. All rational enough, except that there are other oddities about Wilsford. At one point, with all the turmoil of the village around him, he is discovered playing patience. After the stress of killing the policeman in the churchyard and reporting to his German masters, he simply goes home and tucks himself up under a blanket with a whisky and soda. It's as though the character was trying to escape into some undefined somewhere else.

Reviewers also tend to describe Wilsford as the 'English traitor'. Charles Barr does this in *Ealing Studios*, and finds a striking image for the manor under siege, with the defenders at their posts upstairs and Wilsford waiting alone on the ground floor to let in the enemy. The house, Barr suggests, 'functions diagrammatically as a map of "England" under attack.' The balance shifts, however, if Wilsford is to be seen not as English traitor but as German patriot, doing a little more towards earning his Iron Cross.

Turville, the location of 'Bramley End' (centre: Patricia Hayes)

In the long run, this makes no great difference: Wilsford is a traitor as far as Nora is concerned, and probably feels like a traitor to the film's audience. Several critics, however, have seen Wilsford as a traitor by reason of class, a typical figure from the shabby 1930s, and that is more relevant. Take Wilsford out of the game, and one is left with the striking unity of the village. The vicar and the lady of the manor, the policeman and the poacher and the postmistress all die bravely, some heroically. It is the elderly in the village who are killed, and the sailor, the two landgirls and the evacuee who fight and survive. But there are no renegades by class or by age: it is over the shot of a sleeping child that its mother talks about 'giving those Germans a bit of their own back'. All in all, the villagers show unexpected resource, acting individually, reacting to any chance that presents itself, rather than waiting for instructions and leadership. This, presumably, is the message Ealing wanted the film to convey; whether it was also an MoI message has to remain an open question.

3
ACTUALITY AND TECHNIQUE

'*The Lion Has Wings* showed how little we commercial producers knew about this new medium,' Balcon wrote in *Michael Balcon's 25 Years in Films*, a celebratory volume published in 1947 and edited by Monja Danischewsky. *The Lion Has Wings* was the piece of patriotic propaganda hastily put together by Alexander Korda during the first weeks of the war; 'this new medium' was documentary.

One of Balcon's solutions to the problem of putting his studio on a war footing, equipping it to deal with a more urgent brand of realism, was to introduce film-makers from documentary: first Cavalcanti, then Harry Watt. 'Cav and Harry Watt came to us not only feeling dissatisfied with the progress they were making in the government unit, but also feeling that their work had reached a stage where it needed developing along the lines of the story film.' Documentary, more particularly documentary as then understood, was by no means the only route to realism, not even necessarily the best, but it was characteristic of Balcon that he should take this direct and practical approach. The problem, as he saw it, then became one of striking a proper balance between the factual elements of a film and its narrative. *Convoy* (1940), he thought, had too much story; *The Foreman Went to France*, *The Next of Kin* and *Nine Men* got it about right. (No mention, one notes, of *Went the Day Well?*)

Cavalcanti (born 1897) was in his forties when he came to Ealing, on the third lap of his career as a wandering film-maker. He had worked with the French avant-garde in the 1920s, then in Britain with Grierson's GPO Unit, where he made films, developed his ideas about the uses of sound, and by all accounts influenced just about everyone and everything. After Ealing, he went on to make films in several European countries and then in his native Brazil. His reputation as a man of influence and ideas may well outlive his actual films as a director; and one of his ideas, certainly, was that there was more to realist cinema than was understood in John Grierson's philosophy, in which sponsorship and the public services played so large a part. In an interview with Elizabeth Sussex (*Sight and Sound*, Autumn 1975), Cavalcanti said that at some point during the 1930s he had actually suggested to Grierson that the movement might be called 'neo-realism'. Grierson argued that he had to deal with governments. ' "The word documentary impresses them as something serious, as something ..." I said, "Yes, as something dusty and something annoying." '

This interview develops Cavalcanti's more than mixed feelings towards Grierson, a tangle of old loyalties and suspicions, even resentments about credits he felt had been denied him, all still rankling more than thirty years after the event. In *Michael Balcon's 25 Years in Films*, he wrote that he was 'ever grateful to the producer who enabled me to come back into the field of fictional film after my long and hard work in the documentary movement.' In the Sussex interview, he called Balcon 'the best producer I ever had'. Balcon, also quoted at length in Elizabeth Sussex's article, returned all the compliments. 'Of all the help I got, his is the help that was the most important ... he was a highly civilised man ... a particularly outstanding figure ... Of all the group there [at Ealing] I would say that Cavalcanti was the most important and the most talented of the people available to talk to and work with.'

Henri Langlois, in a characteristically beguiling tribute, once said of Cavalcanti that he was 'a man from the eighteenth century who has

Alberto Cavalcanti

strayed into the twentieth century; and what is more, he makes films.' Cavalcanti described himself as 'a surrealist with a tendency towards realism'. He is on record as abominating Gracie Fields, the big star of Ealing before Balcon. The first feature credits Ealing gave him (although he also made documentaries at the studio) were as consultant art director on *The Ghost of St Michael's*, with Will Hay, and *Turned Out Nice Again*, with George Formby. This might seem to add its own touch of surrealism. He was then associate producer on *The Big Blockade* and *The Foreman Went to France*, directed *Went the Day Well?*, was associate producer on *Halfway House* (1943), and did not direct for Ealing again until *Champagne Charlie* (1944) and his dazzling episode in *Dead of Night* (1945). 'I always thought that Cavalcanti was better producer material than he was director material,' Balcon told Elizabeth Sussex, 'though most producers always want to be directors.'

For Sidney Cole, his editor on *Went the Day Well?*, Cavalcanti's influence at Ealing was largely a matter of trying to achieve 'consistency of style'. Danischewsky called him 'the nanny who brought us up'. Michael Relph, half of the Relph-Dearden team of later years, was then a young art director at Ealing and worked as assistant on *Went the Day Well?* and as art director on *The Bells Go Down*, a film about the fire service which immediately followed it into the studio. Relph suggested to me that Cavalcanti probably helped to shift the direction of Ealing war films, that without his influence there could have been a few more like *Ships with Wings*, a film no one then at the studio seems able to mention without a shudder. Also that as 'a bit of a Macchiavellian intriguer, although very sympathetic', he became, or perhaps was merely assumed to be, the person film-makers wanted on their side when seeking Balcon's approval for their projects.

And he was, of course, a theorist and a talker, with the added advantage for the purpose of impressing British colleagues that he still retained a strong foreign accent, liable to become almost incomprehensible at moments of excitement. For a time, Relph says, he foxed them with talk of a film called 'Withering Eats'. Danischewsky tells a pleasing story in his entertaining autobiography, *White Russian, Red Face*. Chan Balcon, Cavalcanti's associate producer, complained that there wasn't enough light in some scenes to see what was going on. (The film was presumably *Went the Day Well?*, although it isn't named.)

Cavalcanti reacted firmly: 'I've been making films in France for years and years where nobody could see nothing and everybody was delighted.' The stray memos from Cavalcanti which survive in the Balcon papers are expressed in entirely lucid terms; either he had a very good secretary, or it was always a matter of the sound rather than the sense.

However Cavalcanti came to *Went the Day Well?*, he went to work on a script which originated in a very different tradition from his own blend of cosmopolitanism, surrealism and documentary experience. Angus MacPhail and John Dighton were old Ealing hands, used to knocking out scripts, no doubt at speed, for George Formby and Will Hay. MacPhail, Diana Morgan suggests, was a good man for ideas but not much of a hand at dialogue; Dighton she remembers sitting quietly in corners mumbling the lines to himself. Diana Morgan herself was Ealing's one resident woman writer during the 1940s, her later credits including *Halfway House, Fiddlers Three, Pink String and Sealing Wax* and *A Run for Your Money*. Not, she says, that Ealing's script credits were entirely to be trusted: 'Sometimes you got a credit for something you hadn't done, or you had written most of the picture and didn't get a credit. We didn't worry about things like that.'

Other women writers came but usually departed, sometimes in tears, put off by the boys' school atmosphere that the studio rather ostentatiously cultivated. To a suggestion some time later that a new woman writer should perhaps be brought in, Robert Hamer countered that he thought they were 'better off with the stale old one we have'. The Ealing tone, Diana Morgan says, tended to be actively hostile towards anything that could be regarded as sentimentality, usually described as 'nauseating'. 'They used to say, "We'll send the Welsh bitch [Morgan] over to put in the nausea."'

Diana Morgan's own training and experience was in the theatre, as a revue writer and West End playwright, and her particular allies at the studio were not the documentarists but film-makers such as Hamer and, later, Alexander Mackendrick. She felt that Ealing 'didn't greatly care for actors, still less actresses,' that for Cavalcanti the players were not much more than 'pawns in a good game'. She saw it as part of her job as writer to try to serve the actors' interests, perhaps to convert pawns into more powerful pieces.

This split of attitude, even understanding about a film's purpose, is not immediately apparent in *Went the Day Well?*, though it may help to explain something about the film's mood and tempo. At the time she was involved in the writing (the final stage, that is), Diana Morgan says that she was working with Angus MacPhail, not at all with Cavalcanti himself. And even meeting her at almost fifty years' remove, it is possible to sense an echo of the sparkiness and stoical good humour that run through the dialogue. 'Sorry, madam, I'm a bit of a heavyweight,' apologises the wounded Sturry as Mrs Fraser hauls him upstairs. 'Don't worry, so am I,' trills back Marie Lohr. 'I don't know when they [the Germans] are more unpleasant, when they're dead or when they're guzzling our rations,' snaps the landgirl Ivy (Thora Hird), bustling about with weapons she has retrieved from German corpses.

Went the Day Well? is unusually and admirably unsentimental. Apart from the casualties in the final battle and the ambush of the four men in the Home Guard, there are a number of close-range killings, in effect acts of murder, carried out by both sides. Not even Wilsford, however, is allowed the luxury of a dying word (the vicar is given one in the shooting script, but it has gone in the film). The film simply steps

Bustling about with weapons: Thora Hird, Elizabeth Allan, Frank Lawton

over the corpses, as it were, disturbing in its matter-of-fact refusal to be deflected from its course.

Yet there are, at the same time, some jolting shifts of mood, which might seem to have more to do with the tone of the script than with a deliberate intention. The villagers, for instance, are allowed three chances to make contact with the outside world. Peggy and Ivy, the two landgirls, scribble a message on an egg, distract their German guard with a lavish helping of pudding and rationed sugar, and press the eggs on a puzzled newspaper boy. The eggs are quickly smashed when the paper boy is knocked off his bicycle by the car driven by Mrs Fraser's Cousin Maud. In the second effort, Mrs Fraser slips a note into Maud's pocket while staging a more sophisticated diversion. This note is also accidentally destroyed.

Both these sequences are almost playful in tone ('Do your stuff, Marlene,' urges Ivy, as Peggy goes to work with the sugar sifter; Cousin Maud is a chatty, breezy woman who teaches housewives how to make the most of a dried egg). They are filmed in a straightforward, businesslike way, with little sense of the slow build-up of constructed, shot-by-shot tension that Hitchcock, for instance, might have managed.

'The eggs are quickly smashed'

The third sequence is entirely different. Mrs Collins (Muriel George), the postmistress, has been established as a forgetful old chatterbox, liable to walk out of her shop still encumbered with her headphones. She drops the telegram announcing Cousin Maud's visit in the village hall, from where it is retrieved scribbled over with the German numerals which first arouse Nora's suspicions. ('I refuse to see anything sinister in an elongated five,' says Mrs Fraser, who clearly finds the vicar's intense daughter something of a trial.) In the evening, Mrs Collins is giving the soldier billeted on her his supper, chattering relentlessly. 'You Germans are partial to sausages ... It's been a pleasant surprise, really, after the way the papers have been carrying on about you Germans sticking babies on the end of bayonets ...' ('Babies on bayonets,' wonders the bemused soldier. 'What would be the advantage?') Has he children? She and her husband never had any. 'Mr Collins blamed me and I blamed him and then he was taken so we never found out ...'

The soldier has been trying to unscrew a recalcitrant pepper pot. (Earlier, she handed it to him with a most meaningful look.) She takes it from him, unscrews it while still talking, flings the pepper in his face. Trying to get up, he knocks the table over and ends on the floor. She reaches for her wood-chopper, stands over him and brings it crashing down – no mere ladylike tap but a full-blooded, two-handed smash. We see no more of the corpse than his hand, lying beside his gun among the shattered teacups. Mrs Collins is allowed an instant of shocked, near-hysterical reaction. Then she is at her switchboard. But the girls at the exchange are chatting: 'That's old mother Collins, she can wait.' Before they answer, she hears the shop bell and turns: another soldier is already moving towards her out of the dark shop with his bayonet fixed. By the time the exchange answers, his hand is reaching out to pull the plug out of the switchboard.

This is a powerful sequence, at least as remarkable as the more celebrated one in which Nora shoots Wilsford. It is quick (about ninety seconds from the opening to the point at which Mrs Collins reaches the switchboard) and it makes its effect through a combination of ruthlessness, a characteristic reticence about actually showing the corpses and the blood, and sheer surprise. In one sense, Mrs Collins might seem the least likely character to be capable of such savage

The German with the
pepper pot

Mrs Collins unscrews it

Pepper thrown in his face

Mrs Collins with the chopper

The German falls to the floor

Mrs Collins telephones for help

The light blinking

The chattering girls at the
exchange

Still calling for help

Mrs Collins is bayoneted

Answering too late

The connection is broken

action; in another, she is one of those old countrywomen who could chatter cheerfully about nothing while wringing the neck of a chicken. The scene is also constructed with a kind of care and deliberation which one doesn't find at too many points in *Went the Day Well?* – the close-up of the soldier's face after the pepper hits him, the shot of Mrs Collins as she walks towards him, taken at ground level so that we see her legs and the chopper dangling in her hand.

Sidney Cole told me two interesting things about the sequence, both demonstrating the extent of Cavalcanti's regard for detail. He had the set built rather smaller than lifesize, to guarantee the cramped, constricted atmosphere he wanted for the killings: violence invading the stuffy little cottage. And he went to the trouble, after shooting on the picture had been completed, to take some extra shots of telephone wires, which are not allowed for in the shooting script. After Mrs Collins plugs in and speaks ('Hullo, Upton, are you there?'), there is a cut to telephone wires, over which her voice can be faintly heard, then to the blinking light on the exchange switchboard ... the girls talking ... back to the wires ... back to Mrs Collins. The effect of the additional shots is certainly a deliberate stretching of the sequence for suspense, although it may now also look like a rather old-fashioned continuity device. Clearly, much care was taken over this sequence; a good deal more, one might suspect, than Cavalcanti took with the other two message attempt scenes.

In a note written for a screening of the film by the Irish Film Society in 1960, Cavalcanti suggested that 'the public enjoyed its pathos and its exceptional violence'. The trouble was 'that when the picture was shown the [invasion] threat no longer existed.' He thought an Irish audience likely to be 'the most capable of understanding its meaning'; which, if more than mere civility, was an odd comment in 1960. And he added a rather forlorn note: after the passage of time, he hoped that 'the difference between the actuality of a subject and the technique of a director would at last be recognised.'

Fifteen years later, when he spoke to Elizabeth Sussex, Cavalcanti was talking about the film in rather a different way. The 'main emphasis' he put on *Went the Day Well?*, according to Mrs Sussex, was its 'deeply pacifist nature'. This on the grounds that 'people of the kindest character, such as the people in that small English village, as soon as war touches them become absolute monsters.' In this, he was being a little hard on his own characters. By the time most of the villagers retaliate, war has done rather more than merely touch them: they have seen their vicar shot down in his own church, the Germans are threatening to shoot some of the children, and they know that the Home Guard men have been 'dealt with'. They are entitled to their outrage, the more so in that this is war at close quarters, in the most familiar of settings, an attack launched by men purporting to be friends and defenders.

There is nothing mealy-mouthed or hesitant, certainly, about the way Bramley End reacts once it has bestirred itself. When the young sailor tackles the guard in the church, in one of Cavalcanti's dimly lit scenes where 'nobody could see nothing', the camera prowls over the crowd of villagers, picking out a woman's excited face. 'That's right, lad, clout him one,' shouts Ivy the landgirl, like someone at a boxing match. Meanwhile Sims, the verger, is down in the boiler room, disposing of another guard with the most cold-blooded and dispassionate efficiency. Later, there is an exchange between the two landgirls, who are firing from the upstairs windows of the manor at the German troops in the garden. 'I ... shot one,' Peggy mutters, pleased but also slightly sickened and dumbfounded. Ivy: 'Good girl. You know, we ought to keep a score. That's one for you. Half a moment now, I'll have a go. Missed him. Can't even hit a sitting Jerry.'

If this sort of thing might seem a little heartless to a generation brought up to take a more tender view of enemy casualties (and to the Cavalcanti of 1975), it was in line with the robustness England expected of its women in these early war years. *Miss Grant Goes to the Door* was a short film made for the MoI by Brian Desmond Hurst in 1940, when the threat of invasion was altogether closer and more urgent. A brisk, tough little film, with an instructional purpose (the front line is in every home; keep your heads) and an energetic story, it concerns two sisters who find a wounded (as it turns out, dying) parachutist on their doorstep and an enemy agent, also in British uniform, flitting about their garden in search of the nearest airfield. Miss Grant (Mary Clare) copes decisively with the emergency, using the dead parachutist's revolver to keep the live German covered, while she sends her sister for help. Won't she be nervous alone with the two Germans? 'One of them is dead,' barks Miss Grant, 'and the other will be if he moves.' She could well have enrolled with the manor house defenders.

In any case, although *Went the Day Well?* retains what may seem like a strict documentary objectivity about the killings, showing no more than a trickle of blood, never lingering over the pain or the bodies, its characters are not all cut from the same cloth. The villager who makes the most personal commitment to violence is no 'monster'. If the film has no hero, the closest it comes to a heroine has to be Nora, the vicar's daughter, if only because she is concerned in the two scenes from the film which everyone seems to remember.

The first is the 'Chocolate' scene, in which George, the spry, inquisitive young evacuee, is rummaging through Hammond/Ortler's kit while Nora tidies his room. 'Funny way to spell chocolate,' he says. Nora glances casually, reprovingly, at what he has unearthed. ' "Chokolade" is the German for chocolate,' she says in the abstracted tone of someone not really listening to a demanding child. And then, suddenly taking in both what she is seeing and what she is saying, 'And "Wien" is the German for Vienna.' Cavalcanti may not have been the greatest director of actors, but he got this scene entirely right.

'Funny way to spell chocolate'

The scene of Wilsford's shooting is by no means the climax to the manor house siege, though it feels like it. On the landing, Tom Sturry is giving the two landgirls a quick lesson in how to use their weapons. Nora picks up one of the German revolvers. 'Think you can handle it?' Sturry asks her. 'Well enough.' Sturry's lesson continues over the shot, as Nora begins to walk slowly down the stairs, as pale and desperate as though she were heading for her own execution. Halfway down, she begins to move rather more quickly and positively: she has made up her mind. She opens the door, throwing a shaft of light across the darkened room. Wilsford is at the barricaded french windows. 'The latch was undone. I was bolting it.' 'Unbolting it,' she says in the coldest of voices. The room itself is in some disorder, furniture strewn about after the building of the barricades, a fitting setting for an extreme action. Wilsford says only 'Nora' as she raises the gun and fires. She is seen in close-up, then Wilsford as he puts his hand to his face. He falls in slow motion. Nora fires two more shots; then, distraught and horrified, also puts her hand to her face.

There, almost brutally, the film leaves her. In a moment, Marie Lohr is being told 'Duck, madam, duck' by Sims, and answering 'I *am* ducking', and the landgirls are firing from the windows. Outside, the British rescuers are advancing into the village. When the British soldiers burst in, the defenders of the manor come stumbling downstairs, but Nora is not with them. Originally, the intention was less ruthless. When the film returns to the churchyard scene of the prologue, with Sims again in peaceful possession of his territory, the camera was to move inside the church for a thanksgiving service. The congregation was to include the villagers we have encountered: Nora and Mrs Fraser (a survivor in the shooting script) standing together, and Tom Sturry and Peggy, who have had time to acquire a small boy old enough to wear a sailor suit. The film's final words were to be taken from the service: 'Thou hast rebuked the heathen, thou hast destroyed the wicked ... Thou hast put out their name for ever and ever. Thou enemy destructions are come to a perpetual end.'

Sidney Cole told me that he was fairly confident this conclusion was never shot; certainly he had no recollection of seeing any footage from it. So the characters are not seen again. Nora, in particular, is abandoned, standing frozen with horror over the man she has killed. As

The shooting of Wilsford

The shooting of Wilsford (continued)

it is, the film ends with Sims' summing up: 'We're proud of ourselves here, proud we had the chance to do our bit, but proudest of all for those who died ... died in the Battle for Bramley End.' Sims taps out his pipe. The camera pulls back from the churchyard, to the road down which it came at the opening of the film. The cast credits come up over the road shot. They are followed by a screen-filling Union Jack, with the words 'A British Picture, made and recorded by Ealing Studios, Ealing, London.' If Cavalcanti in 1942 had any feeling that he had made a pacifist film, and Sidney Cole assures me that he did not, this would have to rate as a decidedly cynical conclusion.

A director has the right, if he chooses, to see his film years later in a different light; and *Went the Day Well?* has of course its basic pacifist credentials. War, as we know, makes people do frightful things. But one of the film's qualities is that it exists within its small, enclosed world of one weekend in one village, not seeming concerned to bring in comments, attitudes and judgments from outside. There is no questioning that the only good German is a dead German. Morale is succinctly defined by George as 'What the wops ain't got.' This, after all, was 1942.

4
THEY CAME IN KHAKI
. . . .

One of the records of the film which survives in the Balcon papers is its budget, which makes instructive reading across the great divide of the years of inflation. The total budgeted cost was £56,486, probably near the average then for a feature on this relatively modest, unstarry scale. Of this, a mere £300 was allocated for the screen rights (though they were, of course, buying the 'idea' rather than the story). Cast costs, including players in crowd scenes, were put at £12,330; set costs at £9,025; everything to do with the music, including payments to the musicians, at £1,000. Cavalcanti's salary amounted to £45 a week for a seventeen-week period.

A separate paper lists the salaries for the actors, initialled by Balcon as though each required his personal approval. Leslie Banks did rather well: £3,000 for thirty-five shooting days, spread over a ten-week period, and £100 a day for any additional time. Marie Lohr was paid £50 a day, with the usual guaranteed minimum number of days; Basil Sydney got £40 a day, Valerie Taylor £30, Mervyn Johns £25. Small part actors, German soldiers and the like, were paid around £7 a day. The War Office was to provide the soldiers (from the Gloucestershire Regiment), with their service transport, weapons and kitbags.

By this stage, the film was ready to go into production, with a ten-week shooting schedule: six weeks in the studio, followed by four weeks on location. It was to be called *They Came in Khaki*, a title evidently arrived at after much dithering. On 5 January 1942, Angus MacPhail sent out a perhaps slightly desperate memo, listing no fewer than twenty titles, with two more following on 20 January. Several of these would surely have sunk any film unlucky enough to sail under them: *Somewhere in England, Incident at Easter, Backwater Battle, Warm Welcome, Off the Map, Right Off the Map, The Heart of the Country*. Other possibilities included *Zero Hour, The Bells Rang, That Saturday Morning, Black Sunday*.

On 27 March, Balcon sent MacPhail a rather exasperated memo. 'As there seems to be no agreement or finality regarding the title ... I have come to the conclusion that *They Came in Khaki* is the best title that has presented itself so far, and *They Came in Khaki* it should remain ... I honestly don't think any useful purpose can be served by continuing the discussion.'

Ealing would seem to have had some problems around this time with titles. Harry Watt's *Nine Men* actually went into production with the amazingly uninviting label of *Umpity Poo* (service slang, it appears, derived from *un petit peu*), before sanity determined otherwise. The battle of *They Came in Khaki* must have rumbled on after the end of shooting, with *Strong in Heart* suddenly putting in a late appearance as an alternative. Balcon noted 'considerable feeling against it', as well he might.

Eventually, they got it right. Or rather, one may conjecture, Balcon himself got it right. The poem from which the title is taken was written anonymously. *Went the Day Well?* was chosen as the title for an anthology of tributes to men and women killed in the war, to which Balcon contributed a memoir of Pen Tennyson, the young rising star of

Ealing, director of *The Proud Valley* and *Convoy*, who was killed in a plane crash in 1941. The book was published in summer 1942, and by 17 July 1942 the title *Went the Day Well?* was also 'perfectly authorised' for the film. To forestall the 'usual criticism' from the press that the studio was unable to make up its mind, it was to be explained that *They Came in Khaki* had been abandoned because 'we did not want to suggest that our story dealt primarily with the enemy. Indeed, it deals mainly with the English villagers.' To round off the title game, the film was released in the United States as *48 Hours*, one of those hardworking movie titles which must have seen service with several films.

It's somehow hard to imagine *They Came in Khaki* surviving fifty years, still less *Strong in Heart*. But how about the film with an alternative cast? A memo of 19 February 1942 throws up some tantalising possibilities: Ralph Richardson as Wilsford; James Mason as Jung, the thuggish German second in command actually played by David Farrar; Edith Evans as lady of the manor; Jimmy Hanley as Tom Sturry; Will Hay as Garbett, the policeman who is murdered by Wilsford during the escape from the church; George Cole instead of Harry Fowler as the young evacuee; Athene Seyler as Cousin Maud; and, more eccentrically, A. E. Matthews as Drew, the local Home Guard commander – though, with that casting, it's hard to imagine Drew earning his living as a baker. Was this ever quite a genuine list of alternatives? In a number of cases, the names seem like the pristine originals of types, represented in the film by less brilliantly defined versions.

As it is, the casting leans heavily towards the soundest and safest of character actors: Marie Lohr, Mervyn Johns, Edward Rigby, Muriel George. None of these would be likely to put a foot wrong, and none does. In the early sequences, before the village wakes up to what has happened to it, there's an awkwardness about some of the establishing scenes, notably those involving Frank Lawton and Elizabeth Allan as the romantic sailor and the landgirl, and also some of the scenes with the soldiers. Balcon felt that language perhaps put up something of a barrier to Cavalcanti's direction of actors. Diana Morgan suggests that he simply didn't like them enough, and remembers one or two of the actors complaining ('though not to him') that they were left too largely to direct themselves. In any case, with the exception of a few isolated scenes, this is hardly an actors' film.

The progress of the shoot can be traced via the weekly reports fed by the studio to the trade press. They began at the end of March 1942 with the vicarage interiors, and had arrived by 15 April at the post-office scene: 'Excellent progress continues to be made.' Rather appealingly, it was reported that some of the actresses were wearing their own clothes; not in the interests of authenticity, but for the sake of wartime economies over clothing coupons. Shooting at the studio did not end until about 20 May, by which time they would have been running a week or so behind schedule. Location shooting went on until the end of June, when it was reported that the unit were back in the studio for the final sequence. This was the scene in the wood involving Edward Rigby and Harry Fowler, for which 'a wood was built on the largest stage'. All in all, a ten-week schedule had stretched to a full three months, which could have some bearing on the way the battle scenes develop.

The main village location was Turville in Buckinghamshire, the manor house being elsewhere. Turville, it seems, was then about as remote and isolated as Potter, though a great deal prettier. The County Council gave Ealing permission to add to the amenities a shop, a house, a porch and a pump, provided these bits and pieces were duly dismantled within two months. Balcon sent his unit into action, it appears, with a schoolmasterly admonition: they should try not to lead innocent villagers astray with their London ways. But according to Diana Morgan, the boot was if anything on the other foot, Turville turning out to be a community of extravagantly wayward habits. A sadder story was told me by Michael Relph. The film unit, as might be expected, drank the Turville pub dry. This being wartime, no further supplies could be delivered until the next quota was due. After the unit left, the villagers set reproachfully on the landlord, an unduly sensitive man who felt so badly about his plight that he killed himself. There are not many traces of Graham Greene surviving in the film; it seems to me that there are rather more in this melancholy tale.

In July, Cavalcanti sent Sidney Cole a diplomatically worded memo asking for some fast work: 'I am frightened that all the warmth and enthusiasm for the picture will wear out if these final stages take too long.' Cole had fairly recently arrived at Ealing as supervising editor, after completing his work with Leslie Howard on *Pimpernel Smith*. Cavalcanti specifically asked for him to be assigned to *Went the Day Well?*. They did not work very closely together, Cole says. 'But if you are a good editor, and I can say that I was, that wouldn't be necessary.' They were sufficiently on the same wavelength.

Sidney Cole made two specific points about the editing, one relevant and one somewhat bizarre. 'You won't,' he said, 'see many people in this film going through doors. We cut on the movement towards the door and then pick them up in the next room.' This was a tactic agreed on with Cavalcanti, to keep the action moving. Early in the film, there is a hilltop scene in which the Home Guard commander obligingly and unsuspectingly points out to Ortler just where he intends to set up machine-gun posts to defend the village. There was so much wind noise on the hill that the scene had to be post-synched. When they came to do this, however, it turned out that Basil Sydney belonged to some religious sect whose members were not allowed to look at their own images. The actor consequently stood sturdily with his back to the screen while recording his dialogue; which did not, as Cole drily commented, make matters easier for the editor.

On 10 August, by which time the film had presumably reached the roughcut stage, Balcon sent Cavalcanti a temperate but critical memo about the way it was going. It was then 10,700 feet, against its eventual registered length of 8,278 feet. Balcon felt that 'further editing must restore to a great extent the mood of urgency which is not yet apparent.' At the outset, he thought, 'the whole thing seems too easy.' There were perhaps too many characters to be introduced and established; too little sense of any real build-up of tension until the 'chocolate' scene. He singled out for comment the message attempt with the eggs and the Cousin Maud sequence (he was 'not in love with the Cousin Maud characterisation'). There was 'no great sense of disappointment when these fail, because they have not been built up sufficiently.' The last reels of the picture were still at a fairly rough stage: 'I believe they will be exciting.'

The production supervisor, John Croydon, sent a memo on the same day. 'I agree with everybody that the film is too long at the moment and that its high spots are rather destroyed by the surplus material between them ... Where sequences have been divided, they could be brought together with improvement to the whole continuity.' The shooting script does chop backwards and forwards between a few sequences, which have been brought together in the film to give a cleaner trajectory.

In the shooting script, the final battle is described as only a rough draft. It would be 'subject to revision according to the advice of our military expert'. And it was noted that the action around the manor house might have to be substantially changed once the location had been chosen. In fact, most of the more significant departures from the shooting script come in this final section, though not all of them have to do with the location or with an expert's advice. It was only at this stage, for instance, that they decided to spare Thora Hird, perhaps already establishing herself as a great survivor, and to dispose of Marie Lohr. ('We enjoyed killing people,' Diana Morgan said, when I asked about reasons for the change.) In the event, the screenwriters allowed the lady of the manor to make a good end, swooping to field a grenade before it explodes in the children's room.

The shooting script envisages a more widespread and more desperate battle, with a good deal of action taking place around the village hall. 'The bodies of dead and wounded British and Germans lie here and there ... There is a gaping hole in the roof of the hall.' In the film, after the army and Home Guard have dealt with the machine-gun posts on the outskirts of the village (the British troops wearing camouflage on their tin hats, so that we can tell attackers and defenders apart), the action centres on the manor. This could be in the interests of economy or because the location they found was such a good one, with a garden in which interesting action could be staged. Gunshots are exchanged amid classically clipped ornamental trees; a German soldier falls among water lilies in a pond. Where matters do become a little sparse is in the actual defence of the manor, effectively entrusted to young Sturry, the two landgirls and the ubiquitous Sims.

Elsewhere, most of the major scenes were filmed much as they were scripted, and the main purpose of a good deal of cutting, trimming and reshuffling was plainly to speed up the action. In particular, to advance the moment, some thirty minutes into the film, when the Germans put 'Plan B' into operation, bewildered hikers are turned back at the barriers in the lanes, the little telephone girl is slapped around to show that the Germans will stand no nonsense, the village settles to its solitary ordeal and the film seems to breathe more freely at the approach of action. Until that point, some of Balcon's criticisms remain valid: a sense of urgency creeps up, but it isn't wound up. And this probably has to do with the shifts of tone, so similar to those in *The Foreman Went to France*, between deadly serious and almost playful. Was this, I asked Diana Morgan, something Cavalcanti positively wanted in the film? Or was he even aware of it? 'I don't think he realised it.' Did she realise it herself, while writing? 'I think I realised that if I had been acting, I would have said ... this is a rotten part.' And, as with *The Foreman Went to France*, energy carries the film over its rough passages.

One still has to look to the shooting script, however, for the explanation of one detail which has always slightly puzzled me. How do the Germans, having just landed by parachute, manage to arrive in the village in their convoy of army trucks? The answer, not surprisingly, is that Wilsford organised the lorries, as one of his many services for his masters in Berlin.

5
A LITTLE TALENT AND TASTE?
· ·

'The critics, led by Miss Lejeune, literally pulled us to pieces,' Cavalcanti wrote in his note for the Irish Film Society screening. In fact, the reviews were by no means all bad, and *Went the Day Well?* had a respectable run at the London Pavilion. But film-makers will always remember the reviews that hurt most, and Caroline Lejeune savaged the film as though she had simply lost her temper with it. She found the action risible, and in her synopsis easily enough managed to make it sound so. 'Any display of hate, except in the hands of an expert director and artist, is to be avoided,' she wrote, 'since high passions without high performance are less likely to lead to conviction than laughter ... The nearer a plot sticks to life at this tense moment of our fortunes, the nearer it gets to drama.' And the boot went in decisively with her final sentence: 'The most patriotic film can lose nothing by the exercise of a little talent and taste.'

Of the two 'Sunday ladies', C. A. Lejeune in the *Observer* would then have carried heavier guns than the relative novice Dilys Powell in the *Sunday Times*. Where the *Observer* spat, the *Sunday Times* quietly praised: 'For once the English people are shown as capable of individual and concerted resourcefulness in a fight and not merely steady in disaster ... The essential virtue of the film is its expression of an English tradition: the tradition of the rural community, self-contained ... still drawing strength from the past, still adding its own experience to the common store of village history ... At last, it seems, we are learning to make films with our own native material.'

But perhaps the most perceptively sympathetic review came from a critic often underrated, now perhaps largely forgotten: William Whitebait (George Stonier) in the *New Statesman*. He got the mood exactly right: 'a mixture of friendly human nature and waking nightmare'. 'It is the sort of film that, after three years of war, with little show and no great expenditure of money, we can make better than anyone. It understates its message, it is beautifully but not too beautifully done, it bridges the gap between ... actors and human beings.' But Whitebait also noted that the film had missed its moment, that 'the temperature is high for invading but low for being invaded', that audiences were in a mood to take calmly events which a year or so earlier they might have found desperately tense. 'Cavalcanti has opened our eyes to reality, even if we may feel that this particular reality is past.'

William Whitebait found reality in the film, Dilys Powell tradition and Caroline Lejeune silly fantasy. Most of the rest lined up to some extent with Lejeune. 'The invasion of this country is not a theme to be treated frivolously,' complained the London *Evening Standard*; the *Scotsman* became rather Scottish about 'an atmosphere of make-believe and childish imagination covering the whole development of the plot'. Even the reviewer in *Documentary News Letter*, though a friend to the film, suggested that it had 'all the appearance of having been made with one eye on the clock and the other on a copy of the *Boys' Own Paper*'.

'Fair average thick-ear fiction for the unsophisticated masses,' summed up the trade paper *Kinematograph Weekly*. 'Out of the rut offering for popular patronage,' decided *Today's Cinema*, after describing the conduct of the Germans as 'scarcely comprehensible at all' and that of the villagers as 'strangely apathetic in the face of national emergency'. The American trade paper *Motion Picture Herald* was severe: 'Candidate only for the most transparent and fantastic type of penny dreadful fiction . . . Scarcely good foreign propaganda for British films.'

Michael Balcon cannot have been best pleased: *The Foreman Went to France* and *The Next of Kin* had by no means been written off as 'thick-ear fiction for the unsophisticated masses'. I have an impression that this was not, in any case, a film Balcon particularly liked. In his papers, there are copies of two lists of the best of Ealing which his office sent out to enquirers: neither includes *Went the Day Well?*, although the films made on either side of it are there – *The Foreman Went to France*, *The Next of Kin*, *Nine Men*, *San Demetrio, London*. Perhaps Lejeune's choleric review rankled. Perhaps Balcon felt, not without reason, that the film had never quite managed to sort out the failings he had noted at roughcut stage. Perhaps he was confirmed in his view that Cavalcanti's best value to his studio was as a producer, someone ideally equipped to influence and help to develop the young Ealing team.

In the end, *Went the Day Well?* remains what it probably always was, the wild card, the joker in the British wartime cinema pack. Increasingly, as the war progressed, films were to become a celebration of duty, and of the comradeship and discipline needed to carry it out. Their heroes were the crews of the *San Demetrio* and the *Torrin (In Which We Serve)*, the army unit of *The Way Ahead*, the fighter squadrons and the bomber crews. In *Went the Day Well?* it could be said that recognised duty dies with the vicar, and his doomed efforts to carry out his responsibility to God, by defending his church against the barbarians, and to country, by ringing the warning bell. (Ironically, one of the Home Guard does actually hear the bell, but they disregard it, on this sleepy Sunday morning, because it would signify the real thing and they know that theirs is only a training exercise.)

After that, it is every man for himself; and just as much, and most unusually for an Ealing war film, every woman for herself. There are no rules, no clearly defined duties and no reassuring orders to be followed, as frightened old women and flighty young ones spur themselves to improvised action – desperate, hopeful, even absurd. The villagers have no choice but to discover a brutality in themselves, which some do more readily than others. Team action begins to develop, though

The ambush of the Home Guard

slowly, as they confront the question of what to do after they have overpowered the guards at the church. The women want to rush to their children, the men immediately to alert the Home Guard. Democratically, they agree to do both.

The contrast between the setting – gentle, peaceful and on the whole virtuous – and the brutish action is ever present, though left unemphasised. (Ortler leaning against the 1914–18 War Memorial while planning his village campaign is the sort of discreet gesture the film allows itself.) But the movie itself is not kindly, gentle or particularly squeamish. It finds its own sustaining virtue in a kind of tough good humour. And, as with so many of the Ealing pictures, it has a sturdy particularity: we are not being invited to look for allegories, to regard Bramley End as a microcosm of England under attack. The village is sufficient to itself: complacent, locked into centuries of peace, quite ready to return to its slumbers as soon as the nightmare is over.

The main criticism at the time was that the film was full of implausible behaviour, mainly by the Germans. By which was meant, I suspect, that the switch between the notion of Germans playing at being British soldiers and unmistakably British actors playing at being German soldiers was not the easiest to carry off persuasively. This, rather than such evident improbabilities as that an officer setting out in command of a secret mission would be allowed to take his sweet ration with him.

If Cavalcanti had wanted to achieve effects of realism and authenticity at all levels of the film, then he should probably have taken an altogether stricter line with the script, pruning it back towards documentary roots, shading it more darkly. (But films, as we know, are seldom made with such strictness, particularly films made in wartime and in a hurry.) The killing of the Home Guard, for instance, is a relentlessly curt and effective episode, shot with a kind of factual economy and conciseness, from the instant when the four men, cheerfully whistling, round the bend on their bikes and head towards the enemy machine-gun and the film's own camera position, to the bundling of the corpses and their gear into the ditch. And then along the road breezes Cousin Maud, with her silly little car and her silly hat.

Perhaps the surrealist side of Cavalcanti was easily able to enjoy such contrasts, to argue that life – or at least life in wartime – may well be like that, even if most sensible movies know better. Or perhaps, as on the whole I think more probable, he simply went ahead and made the film, with all its evident inconsistencies. And, paradoxically, it is just these incongruities and inconsistencies which seem, in the long run, to work to the film's advantage.

Went the Day Well? is not the grim, strenuously 'realistic' study of a village under occupation which might have won more immediate approval from the critics. It is something altogether odder and more untidy: cheerfulness keeps breaking in. The story deals in betrayal, disillusionment, desperate extremes, but the resilience of tone makes it appear that such things are no more than aberrations, disagreeable but not permanently damaging. If Britain had in fact been close to invasion in 1942, *Went the Day Well?* might have looked like a warning against the sort of mentality that would hear the church bell but decide it could safely be ignored. But already by spring 1942, whatever policy the Ministry of Information was still arguing about for its leaflets, the film was dealing with history which hadn't happened and was not going to happen. The realities of war had moved on, and Ealing went on to produce *Nine Men* and *San Demetrio, London*. Unlike these and many of the other war films, with their firmer basis in fact, *Went the Day Well?* had a kind of freedom to make itself up as it went along, rather as Bramley End has to take its fate into its own hands. Even the film's structure sets it out for what it is: imagined history posing as real history, but also aware that the pretence takes in no one.

A postscript. Both Diana Morgan and Mervyn Johns now live at Denville Hall, in Northwood, along with other retired actors and theatre people. 'But, Diana, you were always *killing* me,' Mervyn Johns said to her, looking back to the days in the 1940s when she was writing the movies and he was acting in them. She didn't kill him in *Went the Day Well?*. The indestructibility of Ealing.

CREDITS

Went the Day Well?

GB
1942
Production company
Ealing Studios
UK trade show
3 November 1942
Distributor (UK)
United Artists
US release
28 June 1944
Distributor (US)
AFE Corporation
(US release title:
48 Hours)
Producer
Michael Balcon
Associate producer
S. C. Balcon
Production supervisor
John Croydon
Production manager
Hal Mason
Location manager
Ronnie Brantford
Director
Alberto Cavalcanti
Assistant director
Billy Russell
2nd assistant director
Muriel Cole
3rd assistant director
Norman 'Spike' Priggen
4th assistant director
Cyril Pope
Screenplay
John Dighton, Diana
Morgan, Angus MacPhail
from their own story, based
on a story by Graham
Greene
Continuity girl
Daphne Heathcote
**Photography
(black and white)**
Wilkie Cooper
Camera operator
Gerald Gibbs

Reporting camera
Douglas Slocombe
Camera assistants
Hal Britten, J. Dean,
Desmond Crowley
Music
William Walton
Music director
Ernest Irving
Editor
Sidney Cole
Art director
Tom Morahan
Assistant art director
Michael Relph
Special effects
Roy Kellino
Stills
Wilfrid Newton,
Eddie Orton
Sound supervisor
Eric Williams
Sound recorder
Len Page
Sound camera operator
Peter Davis
Boom operator
Bert Minnell
92 minutes
8278 feet

Leslie Banks
Oliver Wilsford
C. V. France
The Vicar
Valerie Taylor
Nora Ashton
Marie Lohr
Mrs Fraser
Harry Fowler
Young George Truscott
Norman Pierce
Jim Sturry
Frank Lawton
Tom Sturry
Elizabeth Allan
Peggy Fry

Thora Hird
Ivy, landgirl
Muriel George
Mrs Collins
Patricia Hayes
Daisy
Mervyn Johns
Charlie Sims
Hilda Bayley
Cousin Maud
Edward Rigby
Bill Purvis, the poacher
Johnny Schofield
Joe Garbett
Ellis Irving
Harry Drew
Philippa Hiatt
Mrs Bates
Grace Arnold
Mrs Owen
Basil Sydney
Major Ortler
David Farrar
Lieutenant Jung
John Slater
German sergeant
Eric Micklewood
Soldier Klotz
James Donald
German corporal
Gerard Heinz
Schmidt
Charles Paton
Harry Brown
Arthur Ridley
Father Owen
Gerald Moore
Johnnie Wade
Anthony Pilbeam
Ted Garbett
Lilian Ellias
Bridget
Kathleen Boutall
Mrs Sturry
Josephine Middleton
Mrs Carter

Mavis Villiers
Violet
Jose Welford
June
Norman Shelley
Bob Owen
Robert McDermott
BBC announcer
Irene Arnold
Mrs Drew

Leslie Gorman
Robert Bradford
Dean Braine
Wyndham Milligan
H. Victor Weske
German soldiers

and the men of the
Gloucestershire Regiment,
by kind permission of the
War Office

Shooting title:
They Came in Khaki

The print of *Went the Day
Well?* in the National Film
Archive derives from
material donated by United
Artists in 1947.

BIBLIOGRAPHY

Aldgate, Anthony, and
Richards, Jeffrey. *Britain Can
Take It* (Oxford: Basil
Blackwell, 1986).
Balcon, Michael.
A Lifetime of Films (London:
Hutchinson, 1969).
Barr, Charles. *Ealing
Studios* (London: Cameron
and Tayleur/David &
Charles, 1977).
Danischewsky, Monja.

White Russian, Red Face
(London: Gollancz, 1966).
Danischewsky, Monja
(ed.). *Michael Balcon's 25
Years in Films* (London:
World Film Publications,
1947).
Falk, Quentin. *Travels in
Greeneland* (London: Quartet
Books, 1984).
Greene, Graham.
'The Lieutenant Died Last'.

Collier's, 29 June 1940.
Reprinted in *The Last Word
and Other Stories*
(Harmondsworth: Penguin,
1991).
Perry, George. *Forever
Ealing* (London: Pavilion/
Michael Joseph, 1981).
Sussex, Elizabeth.
'Cavalcanti in England'.
Sight and Sound, Autumn
1975, pp. 205–11.

Each book in the BFI Film Classics series honours a great film from the history of world cinema. With four new titles published each spring and autumn, the series will rapidly build into a collection representing some of the best writing on film. Forthcoming titles include *Citizen Kane* by Laura Mulvey, *The Big Heat* by Colin McArthur, *Brief Encounter* by Richard Dyer and *L'Atalante* by Marina Warner.

If you would like to receive further information about future BFI Film Classics or about other books on film, media and popular culture from BFI Publishing, please fill in your name and address below and return the card to the BFI.

No stamp is needed if posted in the United Kingdom, Channel Islands, or Isle of Man.

NAME

ADDRESS

POSTCODE

**BFI Publishing
21 Stephen Street
FREEPOST 7
LONDON
W1E 4AN**